Sonshine

by Emma Cladis

Illustrations
by her Dad

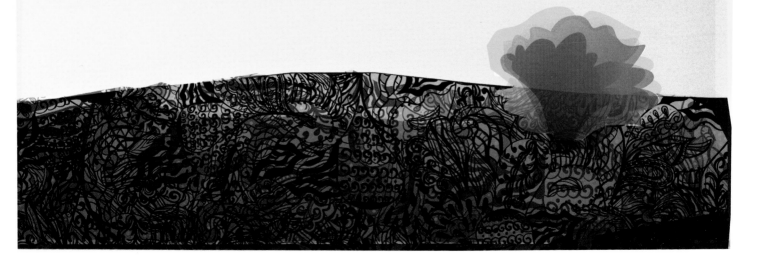

Sonshine

© 2016 Hope Never Ending

All rights reserved. No portion of this book may be reproduced in
any form without the express written consent of the publisher.

For inquiries, sales, or permissions
requests, contact the publisher: hopeneverending.com

Illustrated by Joe Cladis

First Edition

ISBN-978-0-9981034-0-2

Published and printed in the United States of America

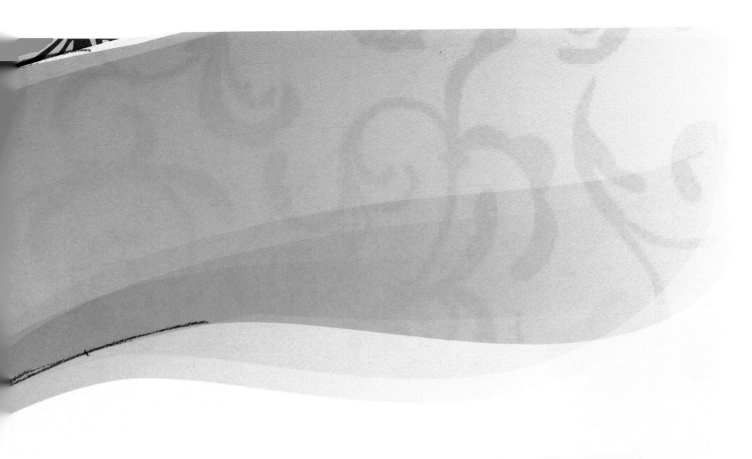

I carried it with me
for many years.
This item brought me hope,
it reminded me I am loved.

Whenever I would
reach for it
and find it with my
finger tips

it assured me everything
would be
alright.

One beautiful morning
I hiked as far and as high up
to a mountain top as I could.

Nature always makes me feel closer to God.

This particular morning
    I needed to feel His presence.
I was on my own,
    hiking, singing, crying.

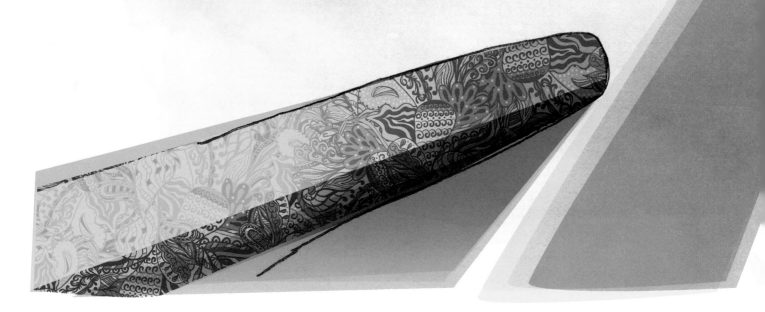

I hiked until my legs
were about to fall off,
then I stopped to sit
on the edge of a cliff
as the sun began to set.

I realized that God
had been hiking with me
all day and that
He was right there with me.

Just like He always is.

As the sun got lower
in the sky the rays
hit some small rocks
I was sitting by.
They looked like a small
pile of gold.

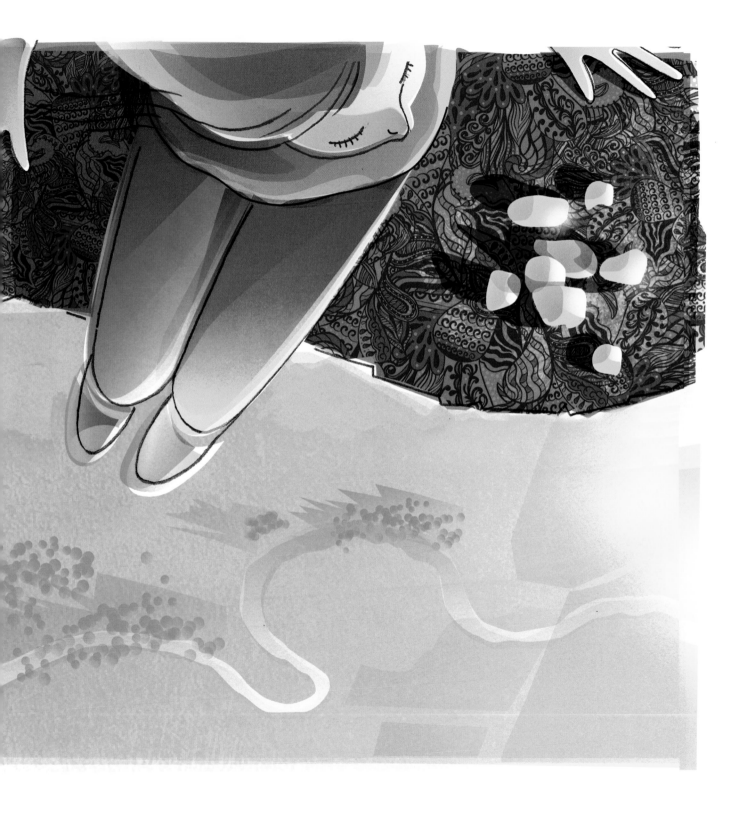

They glistened in
the streams of sun.

Remembering I needed to get
down the mountain before
it was dark, I grabbed one of the
pieces of gold, threw it in my
pocket and started running.

I made it home in plenty of time.

The next day
I found that nugget
   in my jeans pocket.

It was not gold

just a normal
     looking rock.

I heard God say to me.

"The rock
is like you."

"Just normal unless
the son shines on you."

"Then you are more
valvable than gold."

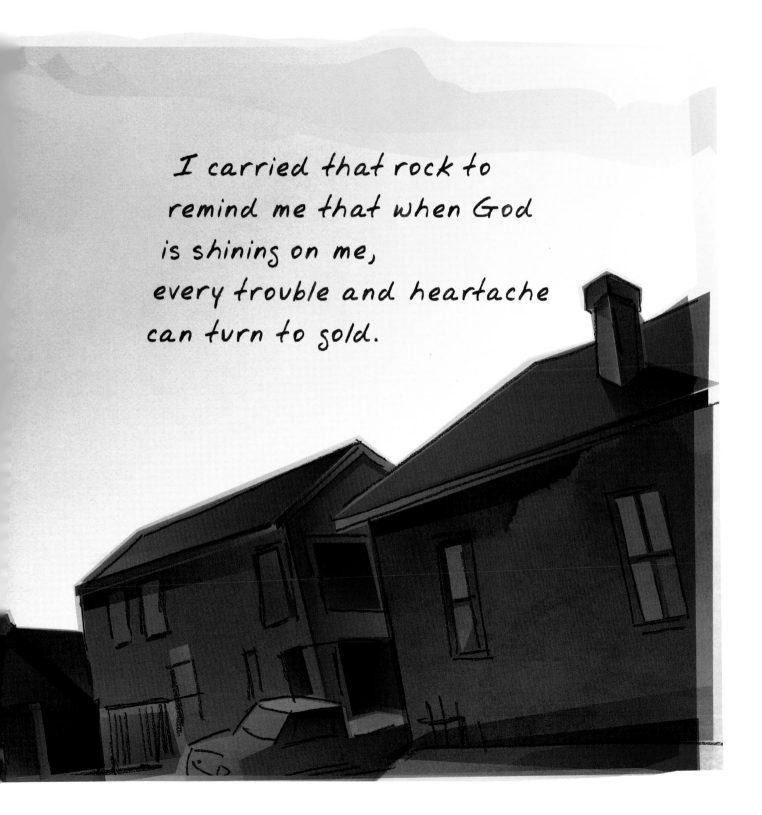

I carried that rock to
remind me that when God
is shining on me,
every trouble and heartache
can turn to gold.

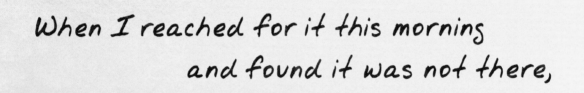

When I reached for it this morning
and found it was not there,

I just smiled,

and realized this loss
will also turn to gold.

And that's why I hope you find it.

So you can be blessed in some way
by that little rock
that taught me so much.

Emma Cladis - Emma is an amazing young woman, she was diagnosed on the autism spectrum when she was two and has been non-verbal most of her life. At six she learned to communicate through typing, which she has used to engage the world ever since. In June 2016 she will graduate, earning her diploma from a main stream high school. For fun, she loves beach walks, swimming in the ocean and socializing with friends. Most of all, Emma is a devoted Christian and loves to write about God and the hope He brings. To learn more about Emma and the other books she is writing, please visit her website, hopeneverending.com.

"Her dad" Joe Cladis - As long as he can remember, Joe has loved to draw. He has spent his life working in the visual arts and is an accomplished art director, graphic designer and illustrator in Southern California. His favorite things to do are being a husband to his lovely wife Karen and Emma's father.